# EVOLUTION OF COMPUTING

## From Logic Gates to Parallel Computers and Beyond

## Dr. Abhinandan H. Patil

**To my Family members, well wishers and Teachers in that order.**

# There is no alternative to hard-work and perseverance

Dr. Abhinandan H. Patil

# TABLE OF CONTENT

# Acknowledgement

Author Acknowledges Kubuntu operating system for providing host based system. HP for great hardware. MathCha for great software for creating this Mathematics Book. Libredraw for creating Diagrams.

Author acknowledges GitHub for providing the great framework for maintaining the code.

# Preface

Please do NOT skip any line. Else the link will be missed and Book will not make sense.

We go on building step by step. We give reference to many Books, Tools and web pages etc. While it is always nice to have self contained Books, the topic is so vast that, we have pointers to references. Second intention is to not repeat what is already mentioned by other Authors. We start with simple computer then move on to 8085/8086/x86 and present day computers. We discuss about systems programming parallel computers. We stop at classical computers. We do not dicuss Quantum computers intentionally. However, some good Books for Quantum computing are mentioned in this Book which can always be referred to.

To re-iterate the focus is classical computers and their evolution and evolution of software along. We dicuss compilers at length. gcc and intel cc are discussed. We restrict the hardware to Intel family of chips because they are widely used. We refer 13 Books in this Book and critically review what is important in each of those Books. How they are relevant to this Book and so on.

**This Book is basically for very advanced users.** Specifically people with advance knowledge of both software and hardware.

# About the Author

Dr. Abhinandan H. Patil is Founder and CTO of Technology Firm in India, Karnataka. Before this, he has worked in Wireless Network Software Organization as Lead Software Engineer for close to a decade. His Research out put is available as Books and Thesis in IJSER, USA. He is Active Researcher in the field of Machine Learning, Deep Learning, Data Science, Artificial Intelligence, Regression Testing applied to Networks, Communication and Internet of Things. He is active contributor of Science, Technology, Engineering and Mathematics. He is currently working on few Undisclosed Books. In the capacity as CTO of organization He carries out Research activity. He has started Blogging recently on Technology and Allied Areas. He is nominated for RULA Research Award in year 2019. He is Adarsh Vidya Saraswati Rashtriya Puraskar Awardee in year 2020. Dr. Abhinandan H. Patil is senior IEEE member since 2013 and is member of Smart Tribe and Cheeky Scientists Association.

Dr. Abhinandan H. Patil can be visited at https://abhinandanhpatil.info and his personal email ID is Abhinandan_patil_1414@yahoo.com

# Chapter 1 Introduction

In this chapter we will be referring few Books dating back to 8080A day ( By Lance A. Leventhal) to current day Quantum Computing Books. We will be having birds view at very high altitude and we will be going into intricacies only when required. I intentionally limit my discussion to Classic Computing and I only give pointers to Quantum Computing. So you can consider referring Books from 1 through 13. 14 onwards it is Quantum computing. Some Books such as Systems Programming by John J Donovan may not be readily available in certain areas. I am aware of that. At many places I will be giving pointers to relevant Books and I dont have intention of replicating the subject content which is already well documented. So the content of my Book may look like review of Books. We start with Logic gates and end at Parallel computers. Following box gives the list of Books that I have referred in this Book. Book should be self contained. However the topic that we are touching upon is so vast, we will be referring the reference Books.

---

**Reference Books**

1. Digital Priciples and Applications by Leach and Malvino
2. Digital Design with An Introduction to Verilog by Morris Mano and Michael
3. 8080A/8085 Assembly level language programming Lance A. Leventhal
4. The 8085 Microprocessors by Uday Kumar and Umashankar
5. Understanding 8085-8086 Microprocessors and Peripherals by S. K. Sen
6. Microprocessor x86 Programming by K R Venugopal and Rajkumar
7. Modern x86 Assembly Language Programming by Daniel Kusswurm
8. Digital System Design with FPGA by Unsalan and Bora Tar
9. Modern VLSI Design by Wayne Wolf
10. Systems Programming by John J. Donovan
11. Compilers Pricples Techniques and Tools by Alfred V Aho and Monica S. Lam
12. Parallel Computer Architecture and Programming by V. Raja Raman & C. Siva Ram Murthy
13. Computer Architecture A Quantitative Approach by Hennessy and Patterson
14. Quantum Computation and Quantum Information by Michael A. Nielsen & Isaac L. Chuang
15. Practical Quantum Computing for Developers by Vladimir Silva
16. Quantum Computing for Computer Scientists by Noson S. Yanofsky and Mirco A. Mannucci

# Chapter 2  Logic Gates and Digital Design

In this chapter we will be referring following Books

1. Digital Priciples and Applications by Leach and Malvino, 7th Edition
2. Digital Design with An Introduction to Verilog by Morris Mano and Michael
3. Digital System Design with FPGA by Unsalan and Bora Tar

and we will be using the following Tools

1. Icarus Verilog version 10.3 (stable) (v10_3)
2. CircuitVerse
3. myHDL implementation in Python

We shall have look at the chapter 16 of Leach and Malvino where Author discusses about A simple computer design. This is **the most** important chapter for us. Building blocks of this computer. They are:

1. Memory
2. Memory Address Register (MAR)
3. Memory Data Register (MDR)
4. Program Counter (PC)
5. Instruction Register (IR)
6. Accumulator (ACC)
7. Timing Counter (TC)
8. Start/Stop Flag (S)
9. **Arithmatic Logic Unit (ALU)**
10. Instruction Decoder (ID)
11. Timing Sequence Decoder (TSD)

Among these

**9. Arithmatic Logic Circuit is Combinatorial Circuit** capable of performing Arithmatic **AND** logic operations. 10 (ID) and 11 (TSD) are 3 to 8 **decoders**. 2 to 8 are **Register Arrays.**
That makes Combinational Logic Circuits(And therefore gates), Data Processing Circuits aka primarily Encoders and Decoders, Arithmatic Circuits, Registers, Memory chapters important for this Book.

The designed simple computer is able to understand 8 Instruction mnemonics. Each

**mnemonic** is one opcode. This understanding is important as micrprocessors etc also work on similar logic. As we shall see the 8085 programs consist of **mnemonics or opcode and operands.**

There are non computing applications like Digital to Analog Converters etc where rest of the chapters of the Book are useful.

## 2.1 What is Verilog?

Now let us say we want to simulate the following combinational logic of Morris Mano Book,

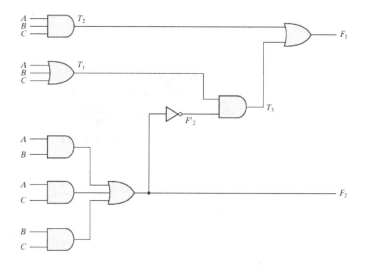

The corresponding Verilog code would look like

Verilog Code for the corresponding Cicruit

```
module Circuit_of_Fig_4_2 (A, B, C, F1, F2);
input A, B, C;
output F1, F2;
wire T1, T2, T3, F2_b, E1, E2, E3;
or g1 (T1, A, B, C);
and g2 (T2, A, B, C);
and g3 (E1, A, B);
and g4 (E2, A, C);
and g5 (E3, B, C);
or g6 (F2, E1, E2, E3);
```

```
not g7 (F2_b, F2);
and g8 (T3, T1, F2_b);
or g9 (F1, T2, T3);
endmodule
// Stimulus to analyze the circuit
module test_circuit;
reg [2: 0] D;
wire F1, F2;
Circuit_of_Fig_4_2 c1 (D[2], D[1], D[0], F1, F2) ;
initial
begin
D = 3'b000;
repeat (7)#10 D = D + 1'b1;
end
initial
$monitor (" ABC = %b F1 = %b F2 = %b ", D, F1, F2);
endmodule
```

**Commands, Outputs and Screen shots**

```
>>iverilog -o my_design Circuit_of_Fig_4_2.v
>>vvp my_design
 ABC = 000 F1 = 0 F2 = 0
 ABC = 001 F1 = 1 F2 = 0
 ABC = 010 F1 = 1 F2 = 0
 ABC = 011 F1 = 0 F2 = 1
 ABC = 100 F1 = 1 F2 = 0
 ABC = 101 F1 = 0 F2 = 1
 ABC = 110 F1 = 0 F2 = 1
 ABC = 111 F1 = 1 F2 = 1
```

```
Morris_mano : bash — Konsole
File   Edit   View   Bookmarks   Settings   Help
(base) abhi@abhi-HP-EliteBook-840-G2:~/AssemblyProgramming/Morris_mano$ iverilog -o my_design Circuit_of_Fig_4_2.v
(base) abhi@abhi-HP-EliteBook-840-G2:~/AssemblyProgramming/Morris_mano$ vvp my_design
ABC = 000 F1 = 0 F2 = 0
ABC = 001 F1 = 1 F2 = 0
ABC = 010 F1 = 1 F2 = 0
ABC = 011 F1 = 0 F2 = 1
ABC = 100 F1 = 1 F2 = 0
ABC = 101 F1 = 0 F2 = 1
ABC = 110 F1 = 0 F2 = 1
ABC = 111 F1 = 1 F2 = 1
(base) abhi@abhi-HP-EliteBook-840-G2:~/AssemblyProgramming/Morris_mano$
```

## Summary:

In this chapter we studied the building blocks of elementary computing circuit. We reviewed the Books that we mentioned in the reference list. We understood why the Books such as Leach and Malvino and Books by Morris Mano are relevant to this Book. We also understood where in the evolution of computing they fit and why they are foundation stones. As an aside topic we studied Verilog and simulated elementary combinational circuit using Tool Icarus. For more infomation on Verilog and VHDL refer Book by Unsulan and Bora Tar.

# Chapter 3 8080A-8085 Microprocessors and 8085 Assembly Programming

Books relevant to this Chapter are:

1. 8080A/8085 Assembly level language programming Lance A. Leventhal
2. The 8085 Microprocessors by Uday Kumar and Umashankar
3. Understanding 8085-8086 Microprocessors and Peripherals by S. K. Sen

Let us have a look at the following figure

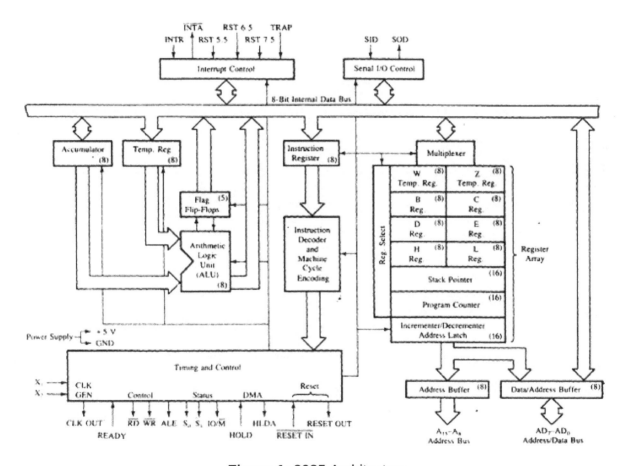

**Figure 1:** 8085 Architecture

Does it resemble simple computer of Chapter 16 of Leach and Malvino, 7th Edition?
Now this 8085 has its own instruction set or mnemonics and accepts the operands to operate upon.

## 3.1 8085 Programming

```
;<Simple program>

jmp start

;data


;code
start: nop

mvi a,23h
mvi b,46h
stc
adc b

mvi a,37h
mvi b,3fh
stc
sbb b

mvi a,37h
stc

hlt
```

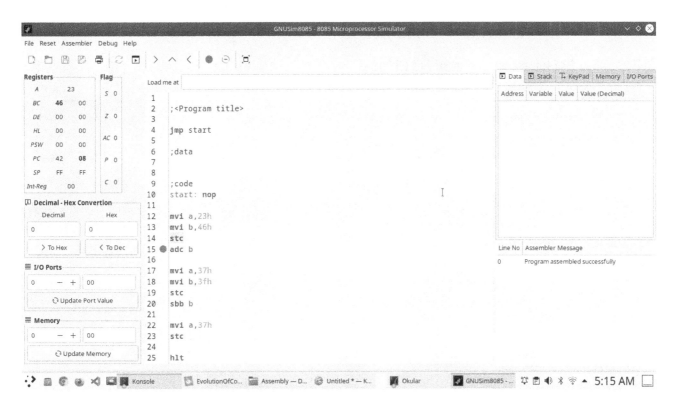

**Figure 2:** 8085 GNU Simulator in Action

This is the stage of evolution of computing when **Assemblers** are actually introduced. Either the human manually translates the mnemonics into hex opcode and keys them in, or human makes use of standard assemblers to translate into Hex bytes. You can also make use of GNU 8085 Simulators etc

## Summary:

We studied 8085 architecture and 8085 programming.

# Chapter 4  8086-80x86 and x86 Programming

Following Books are relevant to this Chapter.

1. Microprocessor x86 Programming by Venugopal and Rajkumar
2. Understanding 8085-8086 Microprocessors and Peripherals by S. K. Sen

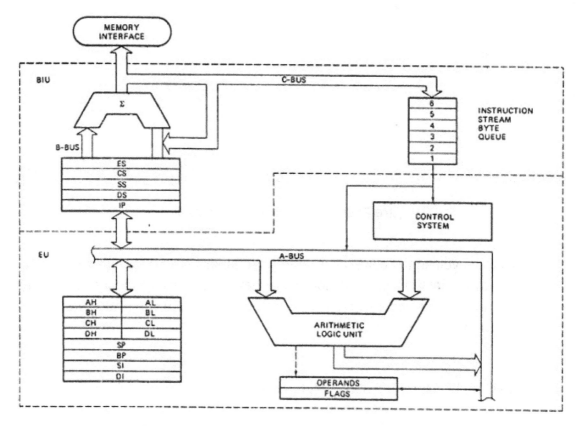

**Figure 3:** 8086 Intel Microprocessor Architecture

Please have a look at the evolution compared to 8085.

Please check out **Wikipedia or other sources** for Intel 80x86 Processors, Pentium Processors etc.  Please check your current processor Architecture. How to check your CPU details ? You should have a utility similar to Display System Information etc on Linux.

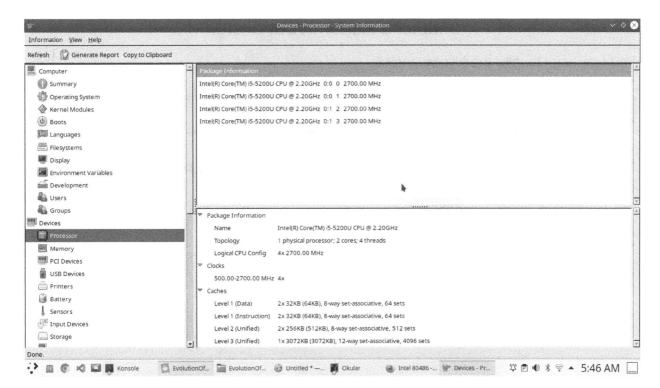

**Figure 4:** Display System Information Utility Details

# Chapter 5 Modern VLSI Design

You may want to refer the following Book:

Modern VLSI Design IP Based Design by Wayne Wolf

Since this Book does not want to be skewed towards hardware, only pointer is given which can be used for further reference.

# Chapter 6 NASM: Microprocessor Programming

We shall take case study NASM on Kubuntu. NASM stands for Netwide Assembler. Basically the assembly programs are non portable. Meaning they are not only hardware specific, for example for a given hardware program written for MASM may not even compile for NASM. For x86_64 assembly program has undergone lot of changes. It is fortunate that we have source like: **https://cs.lmu.edu/~ray/notes/nasmtutorial/**

1. https://cs.lmu.edu/~ray/notes/nasmtutorial/
2. NASM aka Netwide Assembler documentation
3. http://www.intel.com/products/processor/manuals/
4. Modern x86 Assembly Language Programming by Daniel Kusswurm

Programs from source **https://cs.lmu.edu/~ray/notes/nasmtutorial/**

```asm
; -------------------------------------------------------------------
; A 64-bit Linux application that writes the first 90 Fibonacci
numbers. To
; assemble and run:
;
;     nasm -felf64 fib.asm && icc fib.o && ./a.out
; -------------------------------------------------------------------


        global  main
        extern  printf

        section .text
main:
        push    rbx                     ; we have to save this since we use it

        mov     ecx, 90                 ; ecx will countdown to 0
```

```
        xor     rax, rax                    ; rax will hold the
current number
        xor     rbx, rbx                    ; rbx will hold the next
number
        inc     rbx                         ; rbx is originally 1
print:
        ; We need to call printf, but we are using rax, rbx, and
rcx. printf
        ; may destroy rax and rcx so we will save these before
the call and
        ; restore them afterwards.

        push    rax                         ; caller-save register
        push    rcx                         ; caller-save register

        mov     rdi, format                 ; set 1st parameter
(format)
        mov     rsi, rax                    ; set 2nd parameter
(current_number)
        xor     rax, rax                    ; because printf is
varargs

        ; Stack is already aligned because we pushed three 8 byte
registers
        call    printf                      ; printf(format,
current_number)

        pop     rcx                         ; restore caller-save
register
        pop     rax                         ; restore caller-save
register

        mov     rdx, rax                    ; save the current number
        mov     rax, rbx                    ; next number is now
current
        add     rbx, rdx                    ; get the new next number
        dec     ecx                         ; count down
        jnz     print                       ; if not done counting, do
  some more
```

```
        pop      rbx                          ; restore rbx before
returning
        ret
format:
        db    "%20ld", 10, 0
```

Professor Ray's website also mentions how to compile and execute

```
abhi@abhi-HP-EliteBook-840-G2:~/AssemblyProgramming/NASM$ nasm -
felf64 fib.asm && icc fib.o && ./a.out
                    0
                    1
                    1
                    2
                    3
                    5
                    8
                   13
                   21
                   34
                   55
                   89
                  144
                  233
                  377
                  610
                  987
                 1597
                 2584
                 4181
                 6765
                10946
                17711
                28657
                46368
                75025
               121393
```

196418
317811
514229
832040
1346269
2178309
3524578
5702887
9227465
14930352
24157817
39088169
63245986
102334155
165580141
267914296
433494437
701408733
1134903170
1836311903
2971215073
4807526976
7778742049
12586269025
20365011074
32951280099
53316291173
86267571272
139583862445
225851433717
365435296162
591286729879
956722026041
1548008755920
2504730781961
4052739537881
6557470319842
10610209857723
17167680177565

```
            27777890035288
            44945570212853
            72723460248141
           117669030460994
           190392490709135
           308061521170129
           498454011879264
           806515553049393
          1304969544928657
          2111485077978050
          3416454622906707
          5527939700884757
          8944394323791464
         14472334024676221
         23416728348467685
         37889062373143906
         61305790721611591
         99194853094755497
        160500643816367088
        259695496911122585
        420196140727489673
        679891637638612258
       1100087778366101931
       1779979416004714189
```

Similarly factorial.asm called from callfactorial.c gives the output:

```
>>nasm -felf64 factorial.asm && gcc -std=c99 factorial.o
callfactorial.c && ./a.out
factorial( 0) = 1
factorial( 1) = 1
factorial( 2) = 2
factorial( 3) = 6
factorial( 4) = 24
```

```
factorial( 5) = 120
factorial( 6) = 720
factorial( 7) = 5040
factorial( 8) = 40320
factorial( 9) = 362880
factorial(10) = 3628800
factorial(11) = 39916800
factorial(12) = 479001600
factorial(13) = 6227020800
factorial(14) = 87178291200
factorial(15) = 1307674368000
factorial(16) = 20922789888000
factorial(17) = 355687428096000
factorial(18) = 6402373705728000
factorial(19) = 121645100408832000
```

Our intention is not to build the expertise in assembly language programming in x86_64, it is to show that NASM works. Credit goes to the website mentioned.

# Chapter 7 Need for Learning Assembly

According to **Chris Lomont**, "Assembly is often used for performance-critical parts of a program, although it is difficult to **outperform** a good C++ compiler for most programmers. Assembly knowledge is useful for debugging code – sometimes a compiler makes **incorrect** assembly code and stepping through the code in a debugger helps **locate** the cause. Code optimizers sometimes make mistakes. Another use for assembly is interfacing with or fixing code for which you have no source code. Disassembly lets you change/fix existing executables. Assembly is necessary if you want to know how your language of choice works under the hood – why some things are slow and others are fast. Finally, assembly code knowledge is indispensable when diagnosing malware."

More at: https://software.intel.com/content/www/us/en/develop/articles/introduction-to-x64-assembly.html

Now the higher level language compilers such as C++ compilers generating incorrect assembly code is less than 1%. But the words of Chris are invaluable

## Chapter 8 Two Different Compilers Two Different Stories

Let us take the following simple code:
Compile it **with NO special flags** etc:

```
include<stdio.h>
#include<stdlib.h>
#include<time.h>
  int main ()
  {
    int maxSize = 1000000;
    int theArray[maxSize];
    int temp = 0;
    // ref to array theArray
    int nElems = 0;
    // number of data items
    int count = 0;
    clock_t start, end;
    double cpu_time_used;
    start = clock();
    for(count = 0; count< maxSize; count++)
    theArray[count] = maxSize-count;

    for(count = 0; count< maxSize; count++)
          printf("%d  ",theArray[count]);
    for (int p =0; p < maxSize; p++)
    {
        for (int q = p; q < maxSize; q++)
        {
              if ( theArray[p] > theArray[q])
              {
                  temp = theArray[p];
                  theArray[p] = theArray[q];
                  theArray[q] = temp;
              }
        }
    }
```

```
    }
    for(count = 0; count< maxSize; count++)
            printf("%d  ",theArray[count]);
    end = clock ();
    cpu_time_used = ((double) (end - start)) / CLOCKS_PER_SEC;
    printf ("CPU TIME USED %f", cpu_time_used);
    return 0;
    // display items again
}                                    // end main()
```

| Compiler | gcc | intelcc aka icc |
|---|---|---|
| Time taken | 2242.80 seconds | 421.41 seconds |

**Summary: Compiler optimization is different for two different compilers. What might be happening ? That is next chapter**

# Chapter 9 Compilers Under the Hood

To asertain what we have been mentioning:

Write a c toy program for elementary school calculator:

```c
#include <stdio.h>
int main()
{
        int a =5;
        int b=6;
        int result=0;
        int choice=0;
        printf("Enter Choice 1 or 2 or 3 \n");
        scanf("%d",&choice);
        switch(choice)
        {
                case 1: result = a+b;
                        break;
                case 2: result = a-b;
                        break;
                case 3: result = a*b;
                        break;
                default: printf("Invalid Choice");
        }
        printf("Calculator Result is: %d \n",result);
}
```

write the following shell scripts for gcc version 9.3.0 (Ubuntu 9.3.0-10ubuntu2) and icc (ICC) 19.1.2.254 20200623

```
$ cat CalCulator.sh
gcc CalCulator.c -S -o CalCulator.S
gcc -c CalCulator.S -o CalCulator.o
gcc CalCulator.o -o CalCulator
```

and

```
cat CalCulator.sh
icc CalCulator.c -S -o CalCulator.S
icc -c CalCulator.S -o CalCulator.o
icc CalCulator.o -o CalCulator
```

**GCC assembly code**

```
    .file   "CalCulator.c"
    .text
    .section    .rodata
.LC0:
    .string "Enter Choice 1 or 2 or 3 "
.LC1:
    .string "%d"
.LC2:
    .string "Invalid Choice"
.LC3:
    .string "Calculator Result is: %d \n"
    .text
    .globl  main
    .type   main, @function
main:
.LFB0:
    .cfi_startproc
    endbr64
    pushq   %rbp
    .cfi_def_cfa_offset 16
    .cfi_offset 6, -16
    movq    %rsp, %rbp
    .cfi_def_cfa_register 6
    subq    $32, %rsp
    movq    %fs:40, %rax
    movq    %rax, -8(%rbp)
    xorl    %eax, %eax
```

```
    movl   $5, -16(%rbp)
    movl   $6, -12(%rbp)
    movl   $0, -20(%rbp)
    movl   $0, -24(%rbp)
    leaq   .LC0(%rip), %rdi
    call   puts@PLT
    leaq   -24(%rbp), %rax
    movq   %rax, %rsi
    leaq   .LC1(%rip), %rdi
    movl   $0, %eax
    call   __isoc99_scanf@PLT
    movl   -24(%rbp), %eax
    cmpl   $3, %eax
    je   .L2
    cmpl   $3, %eax
    jg   .L3
    cmpl   $1, %eax
    je   .L4
    cmpl   $2, %eax
    je   .L5
    jmp   .L3
.L4:
    movl   -16(%rbp), %edx
    movl   -12(%rbp), %eax
    addl   %edx, %eax
    movl   %eax, -20(%rbp)
    jmp   .L6
.L5:
    movl   -16(%rbp), %eax
    subl   -12(%rbp), %eax
    movl   %eax, -20(%rbp)
    jmp   .L6
.L2:
    movl   -16(%rbp), %eax
    imull   -12(%rbp), %eax
    movl   %eax, -20(%rbp)
    jmp   .L6
.L3:
    leaq   .LC2(%rip), %rdi
```

```
  movl   $0, %eax
  call   printf@PLT
.L6:
  movl   -20(%rbp), %eax
  movl   %eax, %esi
  leaq   .LC3(%rip), %rdi
  movl   $0, %eax
  call   printf@PLT
  movl   $0, %eax
  movq   -8(%rbp), %rcx
  xorq   %fs:40, %rcx
  je     .L8
  call   __stack_chk_fail@PLT
.L8:
  leave
  .cfi_def_cfa 7, 8
  ret
  .cfi_endproc
.LFE0:
  .size   main, .-main
  .ident   "GCC: (Ubuntu 9.3.0-10ubuntu2) 9.3.0"
  .section   .note.GNU-stack,"",@progbits
  .section   .note.gnu.property,"a"
  .align 8
  .long   1f - 0f
  .long   4f - 1f
  .long   5
0:
  .string   "GNU"
1:
  .align 8
  .long   0xc0000002
  .long   3f - 2f
2:
  .long   0x3
3:
  .align 8
4:
```

**Icc assembly code**

```
# mark_description "Intel(R) C Intel(R) 64 Compiler for
applications running on Intel(R) 64, Version 19.1.2.254 Build
20200623";
# mark_description "-S -o CalCulator.S";
    .file "CalCulator.c"
    .text
..TXTST0:
.L_2__routine_start_main_0:
# -- Begin  main
    .text
# mark_begin;
        .align     16,0x90
    .globl main
# --- main()
main:
..B1.1:                             # Preds ..B1.0
                                    # Execution count [1.00e+00]

    .cfi_startproc
..___tag_value_main.1:
..L2:
                                                            #3.1

        pushq      %rbp
#3.1
    .cfi_def_cfa_offset 16
        movq       %rsp, %rbp
#3.1
    .cfi_def_cfa 6, 16
    .cfi_offset 6, -16
        andq       $-128, %rsp
#3.1
        pushq      %r15
#3.1
        subq       $120, %rsp
#3.1
        movl       $3, %edi
#3.1
```

```
        xorl        %esi, %esi
#3.1
        call        __intel_new_feature_proc_init
#3.1
    .cfi_escape 0x10, 0x0f, 0x0e, 0x38, 0x1c, 0x0d, 0x80, 0xff,
0xff, 0xff, 0x1a, 0x0d, 0xf8, 0xff, 0xff, 0xff, 0x22
                                # LOE rbx r12 r13 r14
..B1.14:                        # Preds ..B1.1
                                # Execution count [1.00e+00]
        stmxcsr     (%rsp)
#3.1
        movl        $il0_peep_printf_format_0, %edi
#8.2
        xorl        %r15d, %r15d
#6.12
        orl         $32832, (%rsp)
#3.1
        ldmxcsr     (%rsp)
#3.1
        call        puts
#8.2
                                # LOE rbx r12 r13 r14 r15d
..B1.2:                         # Preds ..B1.14
                                # Execution count [1.00e+00]
        movl        $.L_2__STRING.1, %edi
#9.2
        movl        $choice.112.0.1, %esi
#9.2
        xorl        %eax, %eax
#9.2
#           scanf(const char *__restrict__, ...)
        call        __isoc99_scanf
#9.2
                                # LOE rbx r12 r13 r14 r15d
..B1.3:                         # Preds ..B1.2
                                # Execution count [1.00e+00]
        movl        choice.112.0.1(%rip), %eax
#10.9
```

```
        cmpl        $1, %eax
#10.9
        je          ..B1.9              # Prob 25%
#10.9

                                        # LOE rbx r12 r13 r14 eax r15d
..B1.4:                                 # Preds ..B1.3
                                        # Execution count [7.50e-01]
        cmpl        $2, %eax
#10.9
        jne         ..B1.6              # Prob 66%
#10.9

                                        # LOE rbx r12 r13 r14 eax r15d
..B1.5:                                 # Preds ..B1.4
                                        # Execution count [2.50e-01]
        movl        $-1, %r15d
#14.11
        jmp         ..B1.10             # Prob 100%
#14.11

                                        # LOE rbx r12 r13 r14 r15d
..B1.6:                                 # Preds ..B1.4
                                        # Execution count [5.00e-01]
        cmpl        $3, %eax
#10.9
        jne         ..B1.8              # Prob 50%
#10.9

                                        # LOE rbx r12 r13 r14 r15d
..B1.7:                                 # Preds ..B1.6
                                        # Execution count [2.50e-01]
        movl        $30, %r15d
#16.11
        jmp         ..B1.10             # Prob 100%
#16.11

                                        # LOE rbx r12 r13 r14 r15d
..B1.8:                                 # Preds ..B1.6
                                        # Execution count [2.50e-01]
        movl        $.L_2__STRING.2, %edi
#18.26
        xorl        %eax, %eax
#18.26
```

```
..___tag_value_main.7:
#        printf(const char *__restrict__, ...)
        call        printf
#18.26
..___tag_value_main.8:
        jmp         ..B1.10        # Prob 100%
#18.26
                                   # LOE rbx r12 r13 r14 r15d
..B1.9:                            # Preds ..B1.3
                                   # Execution count [2.50e-01]
        movl        $11, %r15d
#12.11
                                   # LOE rbx r12 r13 r14 r15d
..B1.10:                           # Preds ..B1.9 ..B1.5 ..B1.7
..B1.8
                                   # Execution count [1.00e+00]
        movl        $.L_2__STRING.3, %edi
#20.2
        movl        %r15d, %esi
#20.2
        xorl        %eax, %eax
#20.2
..___tag_value_main.9:
#        printf(const char *__restrict__, ...)
        call        printf
#20.2
..___tag_value_main.10:
                                   # LOE rbx r12 r13 r14
..B1.11:                           # Preds ..B1.10
                                   # Execution count [1.00e+00]
        xorl        %eax, %eax
#21.1
        addq        $120, %rsp
#21.1
.cfi_restore 15
        popq        %r15
#21.1
        movq        %rbp, %rsp
#21.1
```

```
        popq        %rbp
#21.1
  .cfi_def_cfa 7, 8
  .cfi_restore 6
        ret
#21.1
        .align    16,0x90
                                # LOE
  .cfi_endproc
# mark_end;
  .type   main,@function
  .size   main, .-main
..LNmain.0:
  .bss
  .align 4
  .align 4
choice.112.0.1:
  .type   choice.112.0.1,@object
  .size   choice.112.0.1,4
  .space 4  # pad
  .section .rodata.str1.4, "aMS",@progbits,1
  .align 4
  .align 4
il0_peep_printf_format_0:
  .long   1702129221
  .long   1749229682
  .long   1701013871
  .long   1864380704
  .long   540156018
  .long   857764463
  .word   32
  .data
# -- End  main
  .section .rodata.str1.4, "aMS",@progbits,1
  .space 2, 0x00   # pad
  .align 4
.L_2__STRING.1:
  .word   25637
  .byte   0
```

```
    .type    .L_2__STRING.1,@object
    .size    .L_2__STRING.1,3
    .space 1, 0x00    # pad
    .align 4
.L_2__STRING.2:
    .long    1635151433
    .long    543451500
    .long    1768908867
    .word    25955
    .byte    0
    .type    .L_2__STRING.2,@object
    .size    .L_2__STRING.2,15
    .space 1, 0x00    # pad
    .align 4
.L_2__STRING.3:
    .long    1668047171
    .long    1952541813
    .long    1377858159
    .long    1819636581
    .long    1936269428
    .long    1680154682
    .word    2592
    .byte    0
    .type    .L_2__STRING.3,@object
    .size    .L_2__STRING.3,27
    .data
    .section .note.GNU-stack, ""
# End
```

ASSEMBLY CODE IS OPTIMISED DIFFERENTLY by DIFFERENT COMPILERS.
COMPILER GENERATED ASSEMBLY CODE OPTIMISATION BETTER LEFT TO
COMPILER DEVELOPERS.

If you are interested in the hexdump of machine dependent target machine code go ahead run hd on final output. Here how it looks for gcc generated code.

```
00000000  7f 45 4c 46 02 01 01 00  00 00 00 00 00 00 00 00  |.ELF............|
```

```
00000010  03 00 3e 00 01 00 00 00  c0 10 00 00 00 00 00 00  |..>.............|
00000020  40 00 00 00 00 00 00 00  08 3a 00 00 00 00 00 00  |@........:......|
00000030  00 00 00 00 40 00 38 00  0d 00 40 00 1f 00 1e 00  |....@.8...@.....|
00000040  06 00 00 00 04 00 00 00  40 00 00 00 00 00 00 00  |........@.......|
00000050  40 00 00 00 00 00 00 00  40 00 00 00 00 00 00 00  |@.......@.......|
00000060  d8 02 00 00 00 00 00 00  d8 02 00 00 00 00 00 00  |................|
00000070  08 00 00 00 00 00 00 00  03 00 00 00 04 00 00 00  |................|
00000080  18 03 00 00 00 00 00 00  18 03 00 00 00 00 00 00  |................|
00000090  18 03 00 00 00 00 00 00  1c 00 00 00 00 00 00 00  |................|
000000a0  1c 00 00 00 00 00 00 00  01 00 00 00 00 00 00 00  |................|
000000b0  01 00 00 00 04 00 00 00  00 00 00 00 00 00 00 00  |................|
000000c0  00 00 00 00 00 00 00 00  00 00 00 00 00 00 00 00  |................|
000000d0  f0 06 00 00 00 00 00 00  f0 06 00 00 00 00 00 00  |................|
000000e0  00 10 00 00 00 00 00 00  01 00 00 00 05 00 00 00  |................|
000000f0  00 10 00 00 00 00 00 00  00 10 00 00 00 00 00 00  |................|
00000100  00 10 00 00 00 00 00 00  15 03 00 00 00 00 00 00  |................|
00000110  15 03 00 00 00 00 00 00  00 10 00 00 00 00 00 00  |................|
00000120  01 00 00 00 04 00 00 00  00 20 00 00 00 00 00 00  |......... ......|
00000130  00 20 00 00 00 00 00 00  00 20 00 00 00 00 00 00  |. ....... ......|
00000140  98 01 00 00 00 00 00 00  98 01 00 00 00 00 00 00  |................|
00000150  00 10 00 00 00 00 00 00  01 00 00 00 06 00 00 00  |................|
00000160  a0 2d 00 00 00 00 00 00  a0 3d 00 00 00 00 00 00  |.-.......=......|
00000170  a0 3d 00 00 00 00 00 00  70 02 00 00 00 00 00 00  |.=......p.......|
00000180  78 02 00 00 00 00 00 00  00 10 00 00 00 00 00 00  |x...............|
00000190  02 00 00 00 06 00 00 00  b0 2d 00 00 00 00 00 00  |.........-......|
000001a0  b0 3d 00 00 00 00 00 00  b0 3d 00 00 00 00 00 00  |.=.......=......|
000001b0  f0 01 00 00 00 00 00 00  f0 01 00 00 00 00 00 00  |................|
000001c0  08 00 00 00 00 00 00 00  04 00 00 00 04 00 00 00  |................|
000001d0  38 03 00 00 00 00 00 00  38 03 00 00 00 00 00 00  |8.......8.......|
000001e0  38 03 00 00 00 00 00 00  20 00 00 00 00 00 00 00  |8....... .......|
000001f0  20 00 00 00 00 00 00 00  08 00 00 00 00 00 00 00  | ...............|
00000200  04 00 00 00 04 00 00 00  58 03 00 00 00 00 00 00  |........X.......|
00000210  58 03 00 00 00 00 00 00  58 03 00 00 00 00 00 00  |X.......X.......|
00000220  44 00 00 00 00 00 00 00  44 00 00 00 00 00 00 00  |D.......D.......|
00000230  04 00 00 00 00 00 00 00  53 e5 74 64 04 00 00 00  |........S.td....|
00000240  38 03 00 00 00 00 00 00  38 03 00 00 00 00 00 00  |8.......8.......|
00000250  38 03 00 00 00 00 00 00  20 00 00 00 00 00 00 00  |8....... .......|
00000260  20 00 00 00 00 00 00 00  08 00 00 00 00 00 00 00  | ...............|
00000270  50 e5 74 64 04 00 00 00  4c 20 00 00 00 00 00 00  |P.td....L ......|
00000280  4c 20 00 00 00 00 00 00  4c 20 00 00 00 00 00 00  |L ......L ......|
00000290  44 00 00 00 00 00 00 00  44 00 00 00 00 00 00 00  |D.......D.......|
000002a0  04 00 00 00 00 00 00 00  51 e5 74 64 06 00 00 00  |........Q.td....|
000002b0  00 00 00 00 00 00 00 00  00 00 00 00 00 00 00 00  |................|
*
000002d0  00 00 00 00 00 00 00 00  10 00 00 00 00 00 00 00  |................|
000002e0  52 e5 74 64 04 00 00 00  a0 2d 00 00 00 00 00 00  |R.td.....-......|
000002f0  a0 3d 00 00 00 00 00 00  a0 3d 00 00 00 00 00 00  |.=.......=......|
00000300  60 02 00 00 00 00 00 00  60 02 00 00 00 00 00 00  |`.......`.......|
00000310  01 00 00 00 00 00 00 00  2f 6c 69 62 36 34 2f 6c  |......../lib64/l|
00000320  64 2d 6c 69 6e 75 78 2d  78 38 36 2d 36 34 2e 73  |d-linux-x86-64.s|
00000330  6f 2e 32 00 00 00 00 00  04 00 00 00 10 00 00 00  |o.2.............|
00000340  05 00 00 00 47 4e 55 00  02 00 00 c0 04 00 00 00  |....GNU.........|
00000350  03 00 00 00 00 00 00 00  04 00 00 00 14 00 00 00  |................|
00000360  03 00 00 00 47 4e 55 00  8a 27 d7 9b 8c 9c c5 49  |....GNU..'.....I|
00000370  f7 72 98 f6 fa a9 3d 19  74 2d 5e e8 04 00 00 00  |.r....=.t-^.....|
00000380  10 00 00 00 01 00 00 00  47 4e 55 00 00 00 00 00  |........GNU.....|
00000390  03 00 00 00 02 00 00 00  00 00 00 00 00 00 00 00  |................|
000003a0  02 00 00 00 09 00 00 00  01 00 00 00 06 00 00 00  |................|
000003b0  00 00 81 00 00 00 00 00  09 00 00 00 00 00 00 00  |................|
000003c0  d1 65 ce 6d 00 00 00 00  00 00 00 00 00 00 00 00  |.e.m............|
000003d0  00 00 00 00 00 00 00 00  00 00 00 00 00 00 00 00  |................|
000003e0  78 00 00 00 20 00 00 00  00 00 00 00 00 00 00 00  |x... ...........|
000003f0  00 00 00 00 00 00 00 00  1a 00 00 00 12 00 00 00  |................|
00000400  00 00 00 00 00 00 00 00  00 00 00 00 00 00 00 00  |................|
00000410  1f 00 00 00 12 00 00 00  00 00 00 00 00 00 00 00  |................|
00000420  00 00 00 00 00 00 00 00  30 00 00 00 12 00 00 00  |........0.......|
```

```
00000430  00 00 00 00 00 00 00 00  00 00 00 00 00 00 00 00  |................|
00000440  46 00 00 00 12 00 00 00  00 00 00 00 00 00 00 00  |F...............|
00000450  00 00 00 00 00 00 00 00  94 00 00 00 20 00 00 00  |............ ...|
00000460  00 00 00 00 00 00 00 00  00 00 00 00 00 00 00 00  |................|
00000470  0b 00 00 00 12 00 00 00  00 00 00 00 00 00 00 00  |................|
00000480  00 00 00 00 00 00 00 00  a3 00 00 00 20 00 00 00  |............ ...|
00000490  00 00 00 00 00 00 00 00  00 00 00 00 00 00 00 00  |................|
000004a0  37 00 00 00 22 00 00 00  00 00 00 00 00 00 00 00  |7..."...........|
000004b0  00 00 00 00 00 00 00 00  00 6c 69 62 63 2e 73 6f  |.........libc.so|
000004c0  2e 36 00 5f 5f 69 73 6f  63 39 39 5f 73 63 61 6e  |.6.__isoc99_scan|
000004d0  66 00 70 75 74 73 00 5f  5f 73 74 61 63 6b 5f 63  |f.puts.__stack_c|
000004e0  68 6b 5f 66 61 69 6c 00  70 72 69 6e 74 66 00 5f  |hk_fail.printf._|
000004f0  5f 63 78 61 5f 66 69 6e  61 6c 69 7a 65 00 5f 5f  |_cxa_finalize.__|
00000500  6c 69 62 63 5f 73 74 61  72 74 5f 6d 61 69 6e 00  |libc_start_main.|
00000510  47 4c 49 42 43 5f 32 2e  37 00 47 4c 49 42 43 5f  |GLIBC_2.7.GLIBC_|
00000520  32 2e 34 00 47 4c 49 42  43 5f 32 2e 32 2e 35 00  |2.4.GLIBC_2.2.5.|
00000530  5f 49 54 4d 5f 64 65 72  65 67 69 73 74 65 72 54  |_ITM_deregisterT|
00000540  4d 43 6c 6f 6e 65 54 61  62 6c 65 00 5f 5f 67 6d  |MCloneTable.__gm|
00000550  6f 6e 5f 73 74 61 72 74  5f 5f 00 5f 49 54 4d 5f  |on_start__._ITM_|
00000560  72 65 67 69 73 74 65 72  54 4d 43 6c 6f 6e 65 54  |registerTMCloneT|
00000570  61 62 6c 65 00 00 00 00  00 00 02 00 03 00 02 00  |able............|
00000580  02 00 00 00 04 00 00 00  02 00 00 00 00 00 00 00  |................|
00000590  01 00 03 00 01 00 00 00  10 00 00 00 00 00 00 00  |................|
000005a0  17 69 69 0d 00 00 04 00  58 00 00 00 10 00 00 00  |.ii.....X.......|
000005b0  14 69 69 0d 00 00 03 00  62 00 00 00 10 00 00 00  |.ii.....b.......|
000005c0  75 1a 69 09 00 00 02 00  6c 00 00 00 00 00 00 00  |u.i.....l.......|
000005d0  a0 3d 00 00 00 00 00 00  08 00 00 00 00 00 00 00  |.=..............|
000005e0  a0 11 00 00 00 00 00 00  a8 3d 00 00 00 00 00 00  |.........=......|
000005f0  08 00 00 00 00 00 00 00  60 11 00 00 00 00 00 00  |........`.......|
00000600  08 40 00 00 00 00 00 00  08 00 00 00 00 00 00 00  |.@..............|
00000610  08 40 00 00 00 00 00 00  d8 3f 00 00 00 00 00 00  |.@.......?......|
00000620  06 00 00 00 01 00 00 00  00 00 00 00 00 00 00 00  |................|
00000630  e0 3f 00 00 00 00 00 00  06 00 00 00 05 00 00 00  |.?..............|
00000640  00 00 00 00 00 00 00 00  e8 3f 00 00 00 00 00 00  |.........?......|
00000650  06 00 00 00 06 00 00 00  00 00 00 00 00 00 00 00  |................|
00000660  f0 3f 00 00 00 00 00 00  06 00 00 00 08 00 00 00  |.?..............|
00000670  00 00 00 00 00 00 00 00  f8 3f 00 00 00 00 00 00  |.........?......|
00000680  06 00 00 00 09 00 00 00  00 00 00 00 00 00 00 00  |................|
00000690  b8 3f 00 00 00 00 00 00  07 00 00 00 02 00 00 00  |.?..............|
000006a0  00 00 00 00 00 00 00 00  c0 3f 00 00 00 00 00 00  |.........?......|
000006b0  07 00 00 00 03 00 00 00  00 00 00 00 00 00 00 00  |................|
000006c0  c8 3f 00 00 00 00 00 00  07 00 00 00 04 00 00 00  |.?..............|
000006d0  00 00 00 00 00 00 00 00  d0 3f 00 00 00 00 00 00  |.........?......|
000006e0  07 00 00 00 07 00 00 00  00 00 00 00 00 00 00 00  |................|
000006f0  00 00 00 00 00 00 00 00  00 00 00 00 00 00 00 00  |................|
*
00001000  f3 0f 1e fa 48 83 ec 08  48 8b 05 d9 2f 00 00 48  |....H...H.../..H|
00001010  85 c0 74 02 ff d0 48 83  c4 08 c3 00 00 00 00 00  |..t...H.........|
00001020  ff 35 82 2f 00 00 f2 ff  25 83 2f 00 00 0f 1f 00  |.5./....%./.....|
00001030  f3 0f 1e fa 68 00 00 00  00 f2 e9 e1 ff ff ff 90  |....h...........|
00001040  f3 0f 1e fa 68 01 00 00  00 f2 e9 d1 ff ff ff 90  |....h...........|
00001050  f3 0f 1e fa 68 02 00 00  00 f2 e9 c1 ff ff ff 90  |....h...........|
00001060  f3 0f 1e fa 68 03 00 00  00 f2 e9 b1 ff ff ff 90  |....h...........|
00001070  f3 0f 1e fa f2 ff 25 7d  2f 00 00 0f 1f 44 00 00  |......%}/....D..|
00001080  f3 0f 1e fa f2 ff 25 2d  2f 00 00 0f 1f 44 00 00  |......%-/....D..|
00001090  f3 0f 1e fa f2 ff 25 25  2f 00 00 0f 1f 44 00 00  |......%%/....D..|
000010a0  f3 0f 1e fa f2 ff 25 1d  2f 00 00 0f 1f 44 00 00  |......%./....D..|
000010b0  f3 0f 1e fa f2 ff 25 15  2f 00 00 0f 1f 44 00 00  |......%./....D..|
000010c0  f3 0f 1e fa 31 ed 49 89  d1 5e 48 89 e2 48 83 e4  |....1.I..^H..H..|
000010d0  f0 50 54 4c 8d 05 26 02  00 00 48 8d 0d af 01 00  |.PTL..&...H.....|
000010e0  00 48 8d 3d c1 00 00 00  ff 15 f2 2e 00 00 f4 90  |.H.=............|
000010f0  48 8d 3d 19 2f 00 00 48  8d 05 12 2f 00 00 48 39  |H.=./..H.../..H9|
00001100  f8 74 15 48 8b 05 ce 2e  00 00 48 85 c0 74 09 ff  |.t.H......H..t..|
00001110  e0 0f 1f 80 00 00 00 00  c3 0f 1f 80 00 00 00 00  |................|
00001120  48 8d 3d e9 2e 00 00 48  8d 35 e2 2e 00 00 48 29  |H.=....H.5....H)|
00001130  fe 48 89 f0 48 c1 ee 3f  48 c1 f8 03 48 01 c6 48  |.H..H..?H...H..H|
```

```
00001140   d1 fe 74 14 48 8b 05 a5   2e 00 00 48 85 c0 74 08   |..t.H.....H..t.|
00001150   ff e0 66 0f 1f 44 00 00   c3 0f 1f 80 00 00 00 00   |..f..D.........|
00001160   f3 0f 1e fa 80 3d a5 2e   00 00 00 75 2b 55 48 83   |.....=....u+UH.|
00001170   3d 82 2e 00 00 00 48 89   e5 74 0c 48 8b 3d 86 2e   |=.....H..t.H.=.|
00001180   00 00 e8 e9 fe ff ff e8   64 ff ff ff c6 05 7d 2e   |........d.....}.|
00001190   00 00 01 5d c3 0f 1f 00   c3 0f 1f 80 00 00 00 00   |...].............|
000011a0   f3 0f 1e fa e9 77 ff ff   ff f3 0f 1e fa 55 48 89   |.....w.......UH.|
000011b0   e5 48 83 ec 20 64 48 8b   04 25 28 00 00 00 48 89   |.H.. dH..%(...H.|
000011c0   45 f8 31 c0 c7 45 f0 05   00 00 00 c7 45 f4 06 00   |E.1..E......E...|
000011d0   00 00 c7 45 ec 00 00 00   00 c7 45 e8 00 00 00 00   |...E......E....|
000011e0   48 8d 3d 1d 0e 00 00 e8   94 fe ff ff 48 8d 45 e8   |H.=.........H.E.|
000011f0   48 89 c6 48 8d 3d 24 0e   ac fe ff ff 8b 45 e8 83   |H..H.=$......E..|
00001200   ac fe ff ff 8b 45 e8 83   f8 03 74 29 83 f8 03 7f   |.....E...t)....|
00001210   30 83 f8 01 74 07 83 f8   02 74 0f eb 24 8b 55 f0   |0...t....t..$.U.|
00001220   8b 45 f4 01 d0 89 45 ec   eb 28 8b 45 f0 2b 45 f4   |.E....E..(.E.+E.|
00001230   89 45 ec eb 1d 8b 45 f0   0f af 45 f4 89 45 ec eb   |.E....E...E..E.|
00001240   11 48 8d 3d d9 0d 00 00   b8 00 00 00 00 e8 4e fe   |.H.=.........N.|
00001250   ff ff 8b 45 ec 89 c6 48   8d 3d d2 0d 00 00 b8 00   |...E...H.=.....|
00001260   00 00 00 e8 38 fe ff ff   b8 00 00 00 00 48 8b 4d   |....8.......H.M|
00001270   f8 64 48 33 0c 25 28 00   00 00 74 05 e8 0f fe ff   |.dH3.%(...t.....|
00001280   ff c9 c3 66 2e 0f 1f 84   00 00 00 00 00 0f 1f 00   |...f...........|
00001290   f3 0f 1e fa 41 57 4c 8d   3d 03 2b 00 00 41 56 49   |....AWL.=.+..AVI|
000012a0   89 d6 41 55 49 89 f5 41   54 41 89 fc 55 48 8d 2d   |..AUI..ATA..UH.-|
000012b0   f4 2a 00 00 53 4c 29 fd   48 83 ec 08 e8 3f fd ff   |.*..SL).H...?..|
000012c0   ff 48 c1 fd 03 74 1f 31   db 0f 1f 80 00 00 00 00   |.H...t.1.......|
000012d0   4c 89 f2 4c 89 ee 44 89   e7 41 ff 14 df 48 83 c3   |L..L..D..A..H..|
000012e0   01 48 39 dd 75 ea 48 83   c4 08 5b 5d 41 5c 41 5d   |.H9.u.H...[]A\A]|
000012f0   41 5e 41 5f c3 66 66 2e   0f 1f 84 00 00 00 00 00   |A^A_.ff.........|
00001300   f3 0f 1e fa c3 00 00 00   f3 0f 1e fa 48 83 ec 08   |............H...|
00001310   48 83 c4 08 c3 00 00 00   00 00 00 00 00 00 00 00   |H...............|
00001320   00 00 00 00 00 00 00 00   00 00 00 00 00 00 00 00   |...............|
*
00002000   01 00 02 00 45 6e 74 65   72 20 43 68 6f 69 63 65   |....Enter Choice|
00002010   20 31 20 6f 72 20 32 20   6f 72 20 33 20 00 25 64   | 1 or 2 or 3 .%d|
00002020   00 49 6e 76 61 6c 69 64   20 43 68 6f 69 63 65 00   |.Invalid Choice.|
00002030   43 61 6c 63 75 6c 61 74   6f 72 20 52 65 73 75 6c   |Calculator Resul|
00002040   74 20 69 73 3a 20 25 64   20 0a 00 00 01 1b 03 3b   |t is: %d ......;|
00002050   40 00 00 00 07 00 00 00   d4 ef ff ff 74 00 00 00   |@...........t...|
00002060   24 f0 ff ff 9c 00 00 00   34 f0 ff ff b4 00 00 00   |$.......4.......|
00002070   74 f0 ff ff 5c 00 00 00   5d f1 ff ff cc 00 00 00   |t...\...]......|
00002080   44 f2 ff ff ec 00 00 00   b4 f2 ff ff 34 01 00 00   |D...........4...|
00002090   14 00 00 00 00 00 00 00   01 7a 52 00 01 78 10 01   |.........zR..x..|
000020a0   1b 0c 07 08 90 01 00 00   14 00 00 00 1c 00 00 00   |................|
000020b0   10 f0 ff ff 2f 00 00 00   00 44 07 10 00 00 00 00   |..../....D......|
000020c0   24 00 00 00 34 00 00 00   58 ef ff ff 50 00 00 00   |$...4...X...P...|
000020d0   00 0e 10 46 0e 18 4a 0f   0b 77 08 80 00 3f 1a 3a   |...F..J..w...?.:|
000020e0   2a 33 24 22 00 00 00 00   14 00 00 00 5c 00 00 00   |*3$"........\...|
000020f0   80 ef ff ff 10 00 00 00   00 00 00 00 00 00 00 00   |................|
00002100   14 00 00 00 74 00 00 00   78 ef ff ff 40 00 00 00   |....t...x...@...|
00002110   00 00 00 00 00 00 00 00   1c 00 00 00 8c 00 00 00   |................|
00002120   89 f0 ff ff da 00 00 00   00 45 0e 10 86 02 43 0d   |.........E...C.|
00002130   06 02 d1 0c 07 08 00 00   44 00 00 00 ac 00 00 00   |........D......|
00002140   50 f1 ff ff 65 00 00 00   00 46 0e 10 8f 02 49 0e   |P...e....F....I.|
00002150   18 8e 03 45 0e 20 8d 04   45 0e 28 8c 05 44 0e 30   |...E. ..E.(..D.0|
00002160   86 06 48 0e 38 83 07 47   0e 40 6e 0e 38 41 0e 30   |..H.8..G.@n.8A.0|
00002170   41 0e 28 42 0e 20 42 0e   18 42 0e 10 42 0e 08 00   |A.(B. B..B..B...|
00002180   10 00 00 00 f4 00 00 00   78 f1 ff ff 05 00 00 00   |........x......|
00002190   00 00 00 00 00 00 00 00   00 00 00 00 00 00 00 00   |................|
*
00002da0   a0 11 00 00 00 00 00 00   60 11 00 00 00 00 00 00   |........`......|
00002db0   01 00 00 00 00 00 00 00   01 00 00 00 00 00 00 00   |................|
00002dc0   0c 00 00 00 00 00 00 00   00 10 00 00 00 00 00 00   |................|
00002dd0   0d 00 00 00 00 00 00 00   08 13 00 00 00 00 00 00   |................|
00002de0   19 00 00 00 00 00 00 00   a0 3d 00 00 00 00 00 00   |.........=.....|
00002df0   1b 00 00 00 00 00 00 00   08 00 00 00 00 00 00 00   |................|
00002e00   1a 00 00 00 00 00 00 00   a8 3d 00 00 00 00 00 00   |.........=.....|
```

```
00002e10  1c 00 00 00 00 00 00 00  08 00 00 00 00 00 00 00  |................|
00002e20  f5 fe ff 6f 00 00 00 00  a0 03 00 00 00 00 00 00  |...o............|
00002e30  05 00 00 00 00 00 00 00  b8 04 00 00 00 00 00 00  |................|
00002e40  06 00 00 00 00 00 00 00  c8 03 00 00 00 00 00 00  |................|
00002e50  0a 00 00 00 00 00 00 00  bd 00 00 00 00 00 00 00  |................|
00002e60  0b 00 00 00 00 00 00 00  18 00 00 00 00 00 00 00  |................|
00002e70  15 00 00 00 00 00 00 00  00 00 00 00 00 00 00 00  |................|
00002e80  03 00 00 00 00 00 00 00  a0 3f 00 00 00 00 00 00  |.........?......|
00002e90  02 00 00 00 00 00 00 00  60 00 00 00 00 00 00 00  |........`.......|
00002ea0  14 00 00 00 00 00 00 00  07 00 00 00 00 00 00 00  |................|
00002eb0  17 00 00 00 00 00 00 00  90 06 00 00 00 00 00 00  |................|
00002ec0  07 00 00 00 00 00 00 00  d0 05 00 00 00 00 00 00  |................|
00002ed0  08 00 00 00 00 00 00 00  c0 00 00 00 00 00 00 00  |................|
00002ee0  09 00 00 00 00 00 00 00  18 00 00 00 00 00 00 00  |................|
00002ef0  1e 00 00 00 00 00 00 00  08 00 00 00 00 00 00 00  |................|
00002f00  fb ff ff 6f 00 00 00 00  01 00 00 08 00 00 00 00  |...o............|
00002f10  fe ff ff 6f 00 00 00 00  90 05 00 00 00 00 00 00  |...o............|
00002f20  ff ff ff 6f 00 00 00 00  01 00 00 00 00 00 00 00  |...o............|
00002f30  f0 ff ff 6f 00 00 00 00  76 05 00 00 00 00 00 00  |...o....v.......|
00002f40  f9 ff ff 6f 00 00 00 00  03 00 00 00 00 00 00 00  |...o............|
00002f50  00 00 00 00 00 00 00 00  00 00 00 00 00 00 00 00  |................|
*
00002fa0  b0 3d 00 00 00 00 00 00  00 00 00 00 00 00 00 00  |.=..............|
00002fb0  00 00 00 00 00 00 00 00  30 10 00 00 00 00 00 00  |........0.......|
00002fc0  40 10 00 00 00 00 00 00  50 10 00 00 00 00 00 00  |@.......P.......|
00002fd0  60 10 00 00 00 00 00 00  00 00 00 00 00 00 00 00  |`...............|
00002fe0  00 00 00 00 00 00 00 00  00 00 00 00 00 00 00 00  |................|
*
00003000  00 00 00 00 00 00 00 00  08 40 00 00 00 00 00 00  |.........@......|
00003010  47 43 43 3a 20 28 55 62  75 6e 74 75 20 39 2e 33  |GCC: (Ubuntu 9.3|
00003020  2e 30 2d 31 30 75 62 75  6e 74 75 32 29 20 39 2e  |.0-10ubuntu2) 9.|
00003030  33 2e 30 00 00 00 00 00  00 00 00 00 00 00 00 00  |3.0.............|
00003040  00 00 00 00 00 00 00 00  00 00 00 00 00 00 00 00  |................|
00003050  00 00 00 00 03 00 01 00  18 03 00 00 00 00 00 00  |................|
00003060  00 00 00 00 00 00 00 00  00 00 00 00 03 00 02 00  |................|
00003070  38 03 00 00 00 00 00 00  00 00 00 00 00 00 00 00  |8...............|
00003080  00 00 00 00 03 00 03 00  58 03 00 00 00 00 00 00  |........X.......|
00003090  00 00 00 00 00 00 00 00  00 00 00 00 03 00 04 00  |................|
000030a0  7c 03 00 00 00 00 00 00  00 00 00 00 00 00 00 00  ||...............|
000030b0  00 00 00 00 03 00 05 00  a0 03 00 00 00 00 00 00  |................|
000030c0  00 00 00 00 00 00 00 00  00 00 00 00 03 00 06 00  |................|
000030d0  c8 03 00 00 00 00 00 00  00 00 00 00 00 00 00 00  |................|
000030e0  00 00 00 00 03 00 07 00  b8 04 00 00 00 00 00 00  |................|
000030f0  00 00 00 00 00 00 00 00  00 00 00 00 03 00 08 00  |................|
00003100  76 05 00 00 00 00 00 00  00 00 00 00 00 00 00 00  |v...............|
00003110  00 00 00 00 03 00 09 00  90 05 00 00 00 00 00 00  |................|
00003120  00 00 00 00 00 00 00 00  00 00 00 00 03 00 0a 00  |................|
00003130  d0 05 00 00 00 00 00 00  00 00 00 00 00 00 00 00  |................|
00003140  00 00 00 00 03 00 0b 00  90 06 00 00 00 00 00 00  |................|
00003150  00 00 00 00 00 00 00 00  00 00 00 00 03 00 0c 00  |................|
00003160  00 10 00 00 00 00 00 00  00 00 00 00 00 00 00 00  |................|
00003170  00 00 00 00 03 00 0d 00  20 10 00 00 00 00 00 00  |........ .......|
00003180  00 00 00 00 00 00 00 00  00 00 00 00 03 00 0e 00  |................|
00003190  70 10 00 00 00 00 00 00  00 00 00 00 00 00 00 00  |p...............|
000031a0  00 00 00 00 03 00 0f 00  80 10 00 00 00 00 00 00  |................|
000031b0  00 00 00 00 00 00 00 00  00 00 00 00 03 00 10 00  |................|
000031c0  c0 10 00 00 00 00 00 00  00 00 00 00 00 00 00 00  |................|
000031d0  00 00 00 00 03 00 11 00  08 13 00 00 00 00 00 00  |................|
000031e0  00 00 00 00 00 00 00 00  00 00 00 00 03 00 12 00  |................|
000031f0  00 20 00 00 00 00 00 00  00 00 00 00 00 00 00 00  |. ..............|
00003200  00 00 00 00 03 00 13 00  4c 20 00 00 00 00 00 00  |........L ......|
00003210  00 00 00 00 00 00 00 00  00 00 00 00 03 00 14 00  |................|
00003220  90 20 00 00 00 00 00 00  00 00 00 00 00 00 00 00  |. ..............|
00003230  00 00 00 00 03 00 15 00  a0 3d 00 00 00 00 00 00  |.........=......|
00003240  00 00 00 00 00 00 00 00  00 00 00 00 03 00 16 00  |................|
00003250  a8 3d 00 00 00 00 00 00  00 00 00 00 00 00 00 00  |.=..............|
```

```
00003260  00 00 00 00 03 00 17 00  b0 3d 00 00 00 00 00 00  |.........=......|
00003270  00 00 00 00 00 00 00 00  00 00 00 00 03 00 18 00  |................|
00003280  a0 3f 00 00 00 00 00 00  00 00 00 00 00 00 00 00  |.?..............|
00003290  00 00 00 00 03 00 19 00  00 40 00 00 00 00 00 00  |.........@......|
000032a0  00 00 00 00 00 00 00 00  00 00 00 00 03 00 1a 00  |................|
000032b0  10 40 00 00 00 00 00 00  00 00 00 00 00 00 00 00  |.@..............|
000032c0  00 00 00 00 03 00 1b 00  00 00 00 00 00 00 00 00  |................|
000032d0  00 00 00 00 00 00 00 00  01 00 00 00 04 00 f1 ff  |................|
000032e0  00 00 00 00 00 00 00 00  00 00 00 00 00 00 00 00  |................|
000032f0  0c 00 00 00 02 00 10 00  f0 10 00 00 00 00 00 00  |................|
00003300  00 00 00 00 00 00 00 00  0e 00 00 00 02 00 10 00  |................|
00003310  20 11 00 00 00 00 00 00  00 00 00 00 00 00 00 00  | ...............|
00003320  21 00 00 00 02 00 10 00  60 11 00 00 00 00 00 00  |!.......`.......|
00003330  00 00 00 00 00 00 00 00  37 00 00 00 01 00 1a 00  |........7.......|
00003340  10 40 00 00 00 00 00 00  01 00 00 00 00 00 00 00  |.@..............|
00003350  46 00 00 00 01 00 16 00  a8 3d 00 00 00 00 00 00  |F........=......|
00003360  00 00 00 00 00 00 00 00  6d 00 00 00 02 00 10 00  |........m.......|
00003370  a0 11 00 00 00 00 00 00  00 00 00 00 00 00 00 00  |................|
00003380  79 00 00 00 01 00 15 00  a0 3d 00 00 00 00 00 00  |y........=......|
00003390  00 00 00 00 00 00 00 00  98 00 00 00 04 00 f1 ff  |................|
000033a0  00 00 00 00 00 00 00 00  00 00 00 00 00 00 00 00  |................|
000033b0  01 00 00 00 04 00 f1 ff  00 00 00 00 00 00 00 00  |................|
000033c0  00 00 00 00 00 00 00 00  a5 00 00 00 01 00 14 00  |................|
000033d0  94 21 00 00 00 00 00 00  00 00 00 00 00 00 00 00  |.!..............|
000033e0  00 00 00 00 04 00 f1 ff  00 00 00 00 00 00 00 00  |................|
000033f0  00 00 00 00 00 00 00 00  b3 00 00 00 00 00 15 00  |................|
00003400  a8 3d 00 00 00 00 00 00  00 00 00 00 00 00 00 00  |.=..............|
00003410  c4 00 00 00 01 00 17 00  b0 3d 00 00 00 00 00 00  |.........=......|
00003420  00 00 00 00 00 00 00 00  cd 00 00 00 00 00 15 00  |................|
00003430  a0 3d 00 00 00 00 00 00  00 00 00 00 00 00 00 00  |.=..............|
00003440  e0 00 00 00 00 00 13 00  4c 20 00 00 00 00 00 00  |........L ......|
00003450  00 00 00 00 00 00 00 00  f3 00 00 00 01 00 18 00  |................|
00003460  a0 3f 00 00 00 00 00 00  00 00 00 00 00 00 00 00  |.?..............|
00003470  df 01 00 00 02 00 0c 00  00 10 00 00 00 00 00 00  |................|
00003480  00 00 00 00 00 00 00 00  09 01 00 00 12 00 10 00  |................|
00003490  00 13 00 00 00 00 00 00  05 00 00 00 00 00 00 00  |................|
000034a0  19 01 00 00 20 00 00 00  00 00 00 00 00 00 00 00  |.... ...........|
000034b0  00 00 00 00 00 00 00 00  9f 01 00 00 20 00 19 00  |............ ...|
000034c0  00 40 00 00 00 00 00 00  00 00 00 00 00 00 00 00  |.@..............|
000034d0  35 01 00 00 12 00 00 00  00 00 00 00 00 00 00 00  |5...............|
000034e0  00 00 00 00 00 00 00 00  47 01 00 00 10 00 19 00  |........G.......|
000034f0  10 40 00 00 00 00 00 00  00 00 00 00 00 00 00 00  |.@..............|
00003500  13 01 00 00 12 02 11 00  08 13 00 00 00 00 00 00  |................|
00003510  00 00 00 00 00 00 00 00  4e 01 00 00 12 00 00 00  |........N.......|
00003520  00 00 00 00 00 00 00 00  00 00 00 00 00 00 00 00  |................|
00003530  6a 01 00 00 12 00 00 00  00 00 00 00 00 00 00 00  |j...............|
00003540  00 00 00 00 00 00 00 00  7e 01 00 00 12 00 00 00  |........~.......|
00003550  00 00 00 00 00 00 00 00  00 00 00 00 00 00 00 00  |................|
00003560  9d 01 00 00 10 00 19 00  00 40 00 00 00 00 00 00  |.........@......|
00003570  00 00 00 00 00 00 00 00  aa 01 00 00 20 00 00 00  |............ ...|
00003580  00 00 00 00 00 00 00 00  00 00 00 00 00 00 00 00  |................|
00003590  b9 01 00 00 11 02 19 00  08 40 00 00 00 00 00 00  |.........@......|
000035a0  00 00 00 00 00 00 00 00  c6 01 00 00 11 00 12 00  |................|
000035b0  00 20 00 00 00 00 00 00  04 00 00 00 00 00 00 00  |. ..............|
000035c0  d5 01 00 00 12 00 10 00  90 12 00 00 00 00 00 00  |................|
000035d0  65 00 00 00 00 00 00 00  bf 00 00 00 10 00 1a 00  |e...............|
000035e0  18 40 00 00 00 00 00 00  00 00 00 00 00 00 00 00  |.@..............|
000035f0  a3 01 00 00 12 00 10 00  c0 10 00 00 00 00 00 00  |................|
00003600  2f 00 00 00 00 00 00 00  e5 01 00 00 10 00 1a 00  |/...............|
00003610  10 40 00 00 00 00 00 00  00 00 00 00 00 00 00 00  |.@..............|
00003620  f1 01 00 00 12 00 10 00  a9 11 00 00 00 00 00 00  |................|
00003630  da 00 00 00 00 00 00 00  f6 01 00 00 12 00 00 00  |................|
00003640  00 00 00 00 00 00 00 00  00 00 00 00 00 00 00 00  |................|
00003650  10 02 00 00 11 02 19 00  10 40 00 00 00 00 00 00  |.........@......|
00003660  00 00 00 00 00 00 00 00  1c 02 00 00 20 00 00 00  |............ ...|
00003670  00 00 00 00 00 00 00 00  00 00 00 00 00 00 00 00  |................|
```

```
00003680  36 02 00 00 22 00 00 00  00 00 00 00 00 00 00 00  |6..."...........|
00003690  00 00 00 00 00 00 00 00  00 63 72 74 73 74 75 66  |.........crtstuf|
000036a0  66 2e 63 00 64 65 72 65  67 69 73 74 65 72 5f 74  |f.c.deregister_t|
000036b0  6d 5f 63 6c 6f 6e 65 73  00 5f 5f 64 6f 5f 67 6c  |m_clones.__do_gl|
000036c0  6f 62 61 6c 5f 64 74 6f  72 73 5f 61 75 78 00 63  |obal_dtors_aux.c|
000036d0  6f 6d 70 6c 65 74 65 64  2e 38 30 35 39 00 5f 5f  |ompleted.8059.__|
000036e0  64 6f 5f 67 6c 6f 62 61  6c 5f 64 74 6f 72 73 5f  |do_global_dtors_|
000036f0  61 75 78 5f 66 69 6e 69  5f 61 72 72 61 79 5f 65  |aux_fini_array_e|
00003700  6e 74 72 79 00 66 72 61  6d 65 5f 64 75 6d 6d 79  |ntry.frame_dummy|
00003710  00 5f 5f 66 72 61 6d 65  5f 64 75 6d 6d 79 5f 69  |.__frame_dummy_i|
00003720  6e 69 74 5f 61 72 72 61  79 5f 65 6e 74 72 79 00  |nit_array_entry.|
00003730  43 61 6c 6c 63 43 75 6c 61 74  6f 72 2e 63 00 5f 5f 46  |CalCulator.c.__F|
00003740  52 41 4d 45 5f 45 4e 44  5f 5f 2e 5f 5f 69 6e 69  |RAME_END__.__ini|
00003750  74 5f 61 72 72 61 79 5f  65 6e 64 00 5f 44 59 4e  |t_array_end._DYN|
00003760  41 4d 49 43 00 5f 5f 69  6e 69 74 5f 61 72 72 61  |AMIC.__init_arra|
00003770  79 5f 73 74 61 72 74 00  5f 5f 47 4e 55 5f 45 48  |y_start.__GNU_EH|
00003780  5f 46 52 41 4d 45 5f 48  44 52 00 5f 47 4c 4f 42  |_FRAME_HDR._GLOB|
00003790  41 4c 5f 4f 46 46 53 45  54 5f 54 41 42 4c 45 5f  |AL_OFFSET_TABLE_|
000037a0  00 5f 5f 6c 69 62 63 5f  63 73 75 5f 66 69 6e 69  |.__libc_csu_fini|
000037b0  00 5f 49 54 4d 5f 64 65  72 65 67 69 73 74 65 72  |._ITM_deregister|
000037c0  54 4d 43 6c 6f 6e 65 54  61 62 6c 65 00 70 75 74  |TMCloneTable.put|
000037d0  73 40 40 47 4c 49 42 43  5f 32 2e 32 2e 35 00 5f  |s@@GLIBC_2.2.5._|
000037e0  65 64 61 74 61 00 5f 5f  73 74 61 63 6b 5f 63 68  |edata.__stack_ch|
000037f0  6b 5f 66 61 69 6c 40 40  47 4c 49 42 43 5f 32 2e  |k_fail@@GLIBC_2.|
00003800  34 00 70 72 69 6e 74 66  40 40 47 4c 49 42 43 5f  |4.printf@@GLIBC_|
00003810  32 2e 32 2e 35 00 5f 5f  6c 69 62 63 5f 73 74 61  |2.2.5.__libc_sta|
00003820  72 74 5f 6d 61 69 6e 40  40 47 4c 49 42 43 5f 32  |rt_main@@GLIBC_2|
00003830  2e 32 2e 35 00 5f 5f 64  61 74 61 5f 73 74 61 72  |.2.5.__data_star|
00003840  74 00 5f 5f 67 6d 6f 6e  5f 73 74 61 72 74 5f 5f  |t.__gmon_start__|
00003850  00 5f 5f 64 73 6f 5f 68  61 6e 64 6c 65 00 5f 49  |.__dso_handle._I|
00003860  4f 5f 73 74 64 69 6e 5f  75 73 65 64 00 5f 5f 6c  |O_stdin_used.__l|
00003870  69 62 63 5f 63 73 75 5f  69 6e 69 74 00 5f 5f 62  |ibc_csu_init.__b|
00003880  73 73 5f 73 74 61 72 74  00 6d 61 69 6e 00 5f 5f  |ss_start.main.__|
00003890  69 73 6f 63 39 39 5f 73  63 61 6e 66 40 40 47 4c  |isoc99_scanf@@GL|
000038a0  49 42 43 5f 32 2e 37 00  5f 5f 54 4d 43 5f 45 4e  |IBC_2.7.__TMC_EN|
000038b0  44 5f 5f 00 5f 49 54 4d  5f 72 65 67 69 73 74 65  |D__._ITM_registe|
000038c0  72 54 4d 43 6c 6f 6e 65  54 61 62 6c 65 00 5f 5f  |rTMCloneTable.__|
000038d0  63 78 61 5f 66 69 6e 69  6c 69 7a 65 40 40 47 4c  |cxa_finalize@@GL|
000038e0  49 42 43 5f 32 2e 32 2e  35 00 00 2e 73 79 6d 74  |IBC_2.2.5...symt|
000038f0  61 62 00 2e 73 74 72 74  61 62 00 2e 73 68 73 74  |ab..strtab..shst|
00003900  72 74 61 62 00 2e 69 6e  74 65 72 70 00 2e 6e 6f  |rtab..interp..no|
00003910  74 65 2e 67 6e 75 2e 70  72 6f 70 65 72 74 79 00  |te.gnu.property.|
00003920  2e 6e 6f 74 65 2e 67 6e  75 2e 62 75 69 6c 64 2d  |.note.gnu.build-|
00003930  69 64 00 2e 6e 6f 74 65  2e 41 42 49 2d 74 61 67  |id..note.ABI-tag|
00003940  00 2e 67 6e 75 2e 68 61  73 68 00 2e 64 79 6e 73  |..gnu.hash..dyns|
00003950  79 6d 00 2e 64 79 6e 73  74 72 00 2e 67 6e 75 2e  |ym..dynstr..gnu.|
00003960  76 65 72 73 69 6f 6e 00  2e 67 6e 75 2e 76 65 72  |version..gnu.ver|
00003970  73 69 6f 6e 5f 72 00 2e  72 65 6c 61 2e 64 79 6e  |sion_r..rela.dyn|
00003980  00 2e 72 65 6c 61 2e 70  6c 74 00 2e 69 6e 69 74  |..rela.plt..init|
00003990  00 2e 70 6c 74 2e 67 6f  74 00 2e 70 6c 74 2e 73  |..plt.got..plt.s|
000039a0  65 63 00 2e 74 65 78 74  00 2e 66 69 6e 69 00 2e  |ec..text..fini..|
000039b0  72 6f 64 61 74 61 00 2e  65 68 5f 66 72 61 6d 65  |rodata..eh_frame|
000039c0  5f 68 64 72 00 2e 65 68  5f 66 72 61 6d 65 00 2e  |_hdr..eh_frame..|
000039d0  69 6e 69 74 5f 61 72 72  61 79 00 2e 66 69 6e 69  |init_array..fini|
000039e0  5f 61 72 72 61 79 00 2e  64 79 6e 61 6d 69 63 00  |_array..dynamic.|
000039f0  2e 64 61 74 61 00 2e 62  73 73 00 2e 63 6f 6d 6d  |.data..bss..comm|
00003a00  65 6e 74 00 00 00 00 00  00 00 00 00 00 00 00 00  |ent.............|
00003a10  00 00 00 00 00 00 00 00  00 00 00 00 00 00 00 00  |................|
*
00003a40  00 00 00 00 00 00 00 00  1b 00 00 00 01 00 00 00  |................|
00003a50  02 00 00 00 00 00 00 00  18 03 00 00 00 00 00 00  |................|
00003a60  18 03 00 00 00 00 00 00  1c 00 00 00 00 00 00 00  |................|
00003a70  00 00 00 00 00 00 00 00  01 00 00 00 00 00 00 00  |................|
00003a80  00 00 00 00 00 00 00 00  23 00 00 00 07 00 00 00  |........#.......|
00003a90  02 00 00 00 00 00 00 00  38 03 00 00 00 00 00 00  |........8.......|
00003aa0  38 03 00 00 00 00 00 00  20 00 00 00 00 00 00 00  |8....... .......|
```

```
00003ab0  00 00 00 00 00 00 00 00  08 00 00 00 00 00 00 00  |................|
00003ac0  00 00 00 00 00 00 00 00  36 00 00 00 07 00 00 00  |........6.......|
00003ad0  02 00 00 00 00 00 00 00  58 03 00 00 00 00 00 00  |........X.......|
00003ae0  58 03 00 00 00 00 00 00  24 00 00 00 00 00 00 00  |X.......$.......|
00003af0  00 00 00 00 00 00 00 00  04 00 00 00 00 00 00 00  |................|
00003b00  00 00 00 00 00 00 00 00  49 00 00 00 07 00 00 00  |........I.......|
00003b10  02 00 00 00 00 00 00 00  7c 03 00 00 00 00 00 00  |........|.......|
00003b20  7c 03 00 00 00 00 00 00  20 00 00 00 00 00 00 00  ||....... .......|
00003b30  00 00 00 00 00 00 00 00  04 00 00 00 00 00 00 00  |................|
00003b40  00 00 00 00 00 00 00 00  57 00 00 00 f6 ff ff 6f  |........W......o|
00003b50  02 00 00 00 00 00 00 00  a0 03 00 00 00 00 00 00  |................|
00003b60  a0 03 00 00 00 00 00 00  24 00 00 00 00 00 00 00  |........$.......|
00003b70  06 00 00 00 00 00 00 00  08 00 00 00 00 00 00 00  |................|
00003b80  00 00 00 00 00 00 00 00  61 00 00 00 0b 00 00 00  |........a.......|
00003b90  02 00 00 00 00 00 00 00  c8 03 00 00 00 00 00 00  |................|
00003ba0  c8 03 00 00 00 00 00 00  f0 00 00 00 00 00 00 00  |................|
00003bb0  07 00 00 00 01 00 00 00  08 00 00 00 00 00 00 00  |................|
00003bc0  18 00 00 00 00 00 00 00  69 00 00 00 03 00 00 00  |........i.......|
00003bd0  02 00 00 00 00 00 00 00  b8 04 00 00 00 00 00 00  |................|
00003be0  b8 04 00 00 00 00 00 00  bd 00 00 00 00 00 00 00  |................|
00003bf0  00 00 00 00 00 00 00 00  01 00 00 00 00 00 00 00  |................|
00003c00  00 00 00 00 00 00 00 00  71 00 00 00 ff ff ff 6f  |........q......o|
00003c10  02 00 00 00 00 00 00 00  76 05 00 00 00 00 00 00  |........v.......|
00003c20  76 05 00 00 00 00 00 00  14 00 00 00 00 00 00 00  |v...............|
00003c30  06 00 00 00 00 00 00 00  02 00 00 00 00 00 00 00  |................|
00003c40  02 00 00 00 00 00 00 00  7e 00 00 00 fe ff ff 6f  |........~......o|
00003c50  02 00 00 00 00 00 00 00  90 05 00 00 00 00 00 00  |................|
00003c60  90 05 00 00 00 00 00 00  40 00 00 00 00 00 00 00  |........@.......|
00003c70  07 00 00 00 01 00 00 00  08 00 00 00 00 00 00 00  |................|
00003c80  00 00 00 00 00 00 00 00  8d 00 00 00 04 00 00 00  |................|
00003c90  02 00 00 00 00 00 00 00  d0 05 00 00 00 00 00 00  |................|
00003ca0  d0 05 00 00 00 00 00 00  c0 00 00 00 00 00 00 00  |................|
00003cb0  06 00 00 00 00 00 00 00  08 00 00 00 00 00 00 00  |................|
00003cc0  18 00 00 00 00 00 00 00  97 00 00 00 04 00 00 00  |................|
00003cd0  42 00 00 00 00 00 00 00  90 06 00 00 00 00 00 00  |B...............|
00003ce0  90 06 00 00 00 00 00 00  60 00 00 00 00 00 00 00  |........`.......|
00003cf0  06 00 00 00 18 00 00 00  08 00 00 00 00 00 00 00  |................|
00003d00  18 00 00 00 00 00 00 00  a1 00 00 00 01 00 00 00  |................|
00003d10  06 00 00 00 00 00 00 00  00 10 00 00 00 00 00 00  |................|
00003d20  00 10 00 00 00 00 00 00  1b 00 00 00 00 00 00 00  |................|
00003d30  00 00 00 00 00 00 00 00  04 00 00 00 00 00 00 00  |................|
00003d40  00 00 00 00 00 00 00 00  9c 00 00 00 01 00 00 00  |................|
00003d50  06 00 00 00 00 00 00 00  20 10 00 00 00 00 00 00  |....... .......|
00003d60  20 10 00 00 00 00 00 00  50 00 00 00 00 00 00 00  | .......P.......|
00003d70  00 00 00 00 00 00 00 00  10 00 00 00 00 00 00 00  |................|
00003d80  10 00 00 00 00 00 00 00  a7 00 00 00 01 00 00 00  |................|
00003d90  06 00 00 00 00 00 00 00  70 10 00 00 00 00 00 00  |........p.......|
00003da0  70 10 00 00 00 00 00 00  10 00 00 00 00 00 00 00  |p...............|
00003db0  00 00 00 00 00 00 00 00  10 00 00 00 00 00 00 00  |................|
00003dc0  10 00 00 00 00 00 00 00  b0 00 00 00 01 00 00 00  |................|
00003dd0  06 00 00 00 00 00 00 00  80 10 00 00 00 00 00 00  |................|
00003de0  80 10 00 00 00 00 00 00  40 00 00 00 00 00 00 00  |........@.......|
00003df0  00 00 00 00 00 00 00 00  10 00 00 00 00 00 00 00  |................|
00003e00  10 00 00 00 00 00 00 00  b9 00 00 00 01 00 00 00  |................|
00003e10  06 00 00 00 00 00 00 00  c0 10 00 00 00 00 00 00  |................|
00003e20  c0 10 00 00 00 00 00 00  45 02 00 00 00 00 00 00  |........E.......|
00003e30  00 00 00 00 00 00 00 00  10 00 00 00 00 00 00 00  |................|
00003e40  00 00 00 00 00 00 00 00  bf 00 00 00 01 00 00 00  |................|
00003e50  06 00 00 00 00 00 00 00  08 13 00 00 00 00 00 00  |................|
00003e60  08 13 00 00 00 00 00 00  0d 00 00 00 00 00 00 00  |................|
00003e70  00 00 00 00 00 00 00 00  04 00 00 00 00 00 00 00  |................|
00003e80  00 00 00 00 00 00 00 00  c5 00 00 00 01 00 00 00  |................|
00003e90  02 00 00 00 00 00 00 00  00 20 00 00 00 00 00 00  |......... .......|
00003ea0  00 20 00 00 00 00 00 00  4b 00 00 00 00 00 00 00  |. ......K.......|
00003eb0  00 00 00 00 00 00 00 00  04 00 00 00 00 00 00 00  |................|
00003ec0  00 00 00 00 00 00 00 00  cd 00 00 00 01 00 00 00  |................|
```

```
00003ed0  02 00 00 00 00 00 00 00  4c 20 00 00 00 00 00 00  |........L ......|
00003ee0  4c 20 00 00 00 00 00 00  44 00 00 00 00 00 00 00  |L ......D.......|
00003ef0  00 00 00 00 00 00 00 00  04 00 00 00 00 00 00 00  |................|
00003f00  00 00 00 00 00 00 00 00  db 00 00 00 01 00 00 00  |................|
00003f10  02 00 00 00 00 00 00 00  90 20 00 00 00 00 00 00  |......... ......|
00003f20  90 20 00 00 00 00 00 00  08 01 00 00 00 00 00 00  |. ..............|
00003f30  00 00 00 00 00 00 00 00  08 00 00 00 00 00 00 00  |................|
00003f40  00 00 00 00 00 00 00 00  e5 00 00 00 0e 00 00 00  |................|
00003f50  03 00 00 00 00 00 00 00  a0 3d 00 00 00 00 00 00  |.........=......|
00003f60  a0 2d 00 00 00 00 00 00  08 00 00 00 00 00 00 00  |.-..............|
00003f70  00 00 00 00 00 00 00 00  08 00 00 00 00 00 00 00  |................|
00003f80  08 00 00 00 00 00 00 00  f1 00 00 00 0f 00 00 00  |................|
00003f90  03 00 00 00 00 00 00 00  a8 3d 00 00 00 00 00 00  |.........=......|
00003fa0  a8 2d 00 00 00 00 00 00  08 00 00 00 00 00 00 00  |.-..............|
00003fb0  00 00 00 00 00 00 00 00  08 00 00 00 00 00 00 00  |................|
00003fc0  08 00 00 00 00 00 00 00  fd 00 00 00 06 00 00 00  |................|
00003fd0  03 00 00 00 00 00 00 00  b0 3d 00 00 00 00 00 00  |.........=......|
00003fe0  b0 2d 00 00 00 00 00 00  f0 01 00 00 00 00 00 00  |.-..............|
00003ff0  07 00 00 00 00 00 00 00  08 00 00 00 00 00 00 00  |................|
00004000  10 00 00 00 00 00 00 00  ab 00 00 00 01 00 00 00  |................|
00004010  03 00 00 00 00 00 00 00  a0 3f 00 00 00 00 00 00  |.........?......|
00004020  a0 2f 00 00 00 00 00 00  60 00 00 00 00 00 00 00  |./......`.......|
00004030  00 00 00 00 00 00 00 00  08 00 00 00 00 00 00 00  |................|
00004040  08 00 00 00 00 00 00 00  06 01 00 00 01 00 00 00  |................|
00004050  03 00 00 00 00 00 00 00  00 40 00 00 00 00 00 00  |.........@......|
00004060  00 30 00 00 00 00 00 00  10 00 00 00 00 00 00 00  |.0..............|
00004070  00 00 00 00 00 00 00 00  08 00 00 00 00 00 00 00  |................|
00004080  00 00 00 00 00 00 00 00  0c 01 00 00 08 00 00 00  |................|
00004090  03 00 00 00 00 00 00 00  10 40 00 00 00 00 00 00  |.........@......|
000040a0  10 30 00 00 00 00 00 00  08 00 00 00 00 00 00 00  |.0..............|
000040b0  00 00 00 00 00 00 00 00  01 00 00 00 00 00 00 00  |................|
000040c0  00 00 00 00 00 00 00 00  11 01 00 00 01 00 00 00  |................|
000040d0  30 00 00 00 00 00 00 00  00 00 00 00 00 00 00 00  |0...............|
000040e0  10 30 00 00 00 00 00 00  24 00 00 00 00 00 00 00  |.0......$.......|
000040f0  00 00 00 00 00 00 00 00  01 00 00 00 00 00 00 00  |................|
00004100  01 00 00 00 00 00 00 00  01 00 00 00 02 00 00 00  |................|
00004110  00 00 00 00 00 00 00 00  00 00 00 00 00 00 00 00  |................|
00004120  38 30 00 00 00 00 00 00  60 06 00 00 00 00 00 00  |80......`.......|
00004130  1d 00 00 00 2e 00 00 00  08 00 00 00 00 00 00 00  |................|
00004140  18 00 00 00 00 00 00 00  09 00 00 00 03 00 00 00  |................|
00004150  00 00 00 00 00 00 00 00  00 00 00 00 00 00 00 00  |................|
00004160  98 36 00 00 00 00 00 00  52 02 00 00 00 00 00 00  |.6......R.......|
00004170  00 00 00 00 00 00 00 00  01 00 00 00 00 00 00 00  |................|
00004180  00 00 00 00 00 00 00 00  11 00 00 00 03 00 00 00  |................|
00004190  00 00 00 00 00 00 00 00  00 00 00 00 00 00 00 00  |................|
000041a0  ea 38 00 00 00 00 00 00  1a 01 00 00 00 00 00 00  |.8..............|
000041b0  00 00 00 00 00 00 00 00  01 00 00 00 00 00 00 00  |................|
*
000041c8
```

# Chapter 10 A Language Processing Systems

Have a look at the following diagram

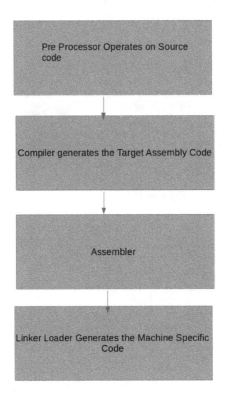

**Figure 5:** A Language processing System

All the Blocks can be correlated with the steps that we did in the last chapter. For further reading refer:

Compilers Priciples, Techniques and Tool by Alfred V. Aho, Monica S. Lam

## Chapter 11   Parallel Computers Architecture and Programming

1. Parallel Computer Architecture and Programming by V. Raja Raman & C. Siva Ram Murthy **OR**
2. Computer Architecture a Quantitative Approach by Hennessy and Patterson

Sections look for:

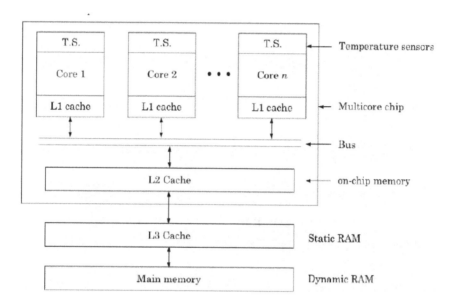

**Figure 6:** MultiCore

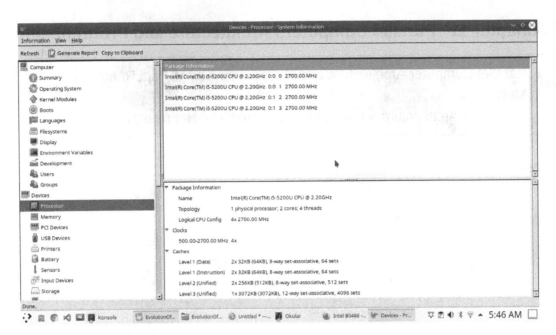

**Figure 7:** System Information

6 and 7 are related. Therefore 7 is repeated. Also check out Instruction level parallel processing and core level parallel processing.

# Chapter 12  Quantum Computers

Few Resources for reference

1. Quantum Computation and Quantum Information by Michael A. Nielsen & Isaac L. Chuang
2. Practical Quantum Computing for Developers by Vladimir Silva
3. Quantum Computing for Computer Scientists by Noson S. Yanofsky and Mirco A. Mannucci

# Chapter 13 Conclusion

We looked at Evolution of computing starting from simple computer involving basic gates to todays Classic Parallel computer with emphasis on assembler and compilers.

Evolution of Computing

www.ingramcontent.com/pod-product-compliance
Lightning Source LLC
Chambersburg PA
CBHW060443060326
40690CB00019B/4319